FIRE TRUCKS
AND RESCUE VEHICLES

Jean Coppendale

School Specialty®
Publishing

Columbus, Ohio

This edition published in the United States in 2009 by Brighter Child, an imprint of School Specialty Publishing, a member of the School Specialty Family.

Send inquiries to:
School Specialty Publishing
8720 Orion Place
Columbus, Ohio 43240

www.SchoolSpecialtyPublishing.com

ISBN 0-7696-5795-8
ISBN 13: 978-0-7696-5795-0
Part Number: M00001005

First published in the United States by
QEB Publishing, Inc.
23062 La Cadena Drive
Laguna Hills, CA 92653

www.qeb-publishing.com

Written by Jean Coppendale
Designed by Rahul Dhiman (Q2A Media)
Editor Katie Bainbridge
Picture Researcher Jyoti Sachdev (Q2A Media)

Publisher Steve Evans
Creative Director Zeta Davies
Senior Editor Hannah Ray

Printed and bound in China.

Picture credits

Key: t = top, b = bottom, c = center,
l = left, r = right, FC = front cover, BC = back cover
Dreamstime: FC/ Corbis: BC; George Hall/ Shutterstock: 4–5; Keith Levit/ Photo Researchers, Inc./ Photolibrary: 5t; Mauritius Die Bildagentur Gmbh/ Photolibrary: 6–7; Micah May/ Shutterstock: 7t; BIOS Gunther Michel/ Still Pictures: 8–9; Markus Dlouhy/ Still Pictures: 9b; Oshkosh Truck Corporation: 10–11; Index Stock Imagery/ Photolibrary: 12–13; Photo Researchers, Inc./ Photolibrary: 13t; Mark William Penny/ Shutterstock: 14–15; LA(Phot) Emma Somerfield/ Royal Navy: 15t; Oshkosh Truck Corporation: 16–17; OEAMTC: 17t; Ford Motor Company: 18–19; Jochen Tack/ Still Pictures: 19t; REUTERS/ Fabrizio Bensch: 20b; REUTERS/ Guido Benschop:20–21

Table of Contents

Words in **bold** can be found in the glossary.

Quick! Emergency!

If there is an accident or if someone is in trouble, an emergency **vehicle** and specially-trained people rush to the scene to help.

Whenever there is a traffic accident or emergency, police officers come out to help.

Fire engines, ambulances, police cars, lifeboats, and rescue helicopters are all emergency vehicles. Most emergency cars and trucks have a **siren** and flashing lights. They let people know to clear the way so the emergency vehicle can get through traffic quickly.

Help! Fire!

Fire engines and fire trucks are used to put out fires. Fire engines have tanks of water and hoses that are used to spray water onto a fire. Fire trucks have long ladders that are used to rescue people from high places. Firefighters wear special uniforms, boots, and helmets to protect themselves from flames, heat, and smoke.

A fire truck has metal stands underneath its body. They are used to help stop the truck from tipping over when the ladder is being used.

Fire truck ladders can be turned in any direction to reach people trapped in high places.

7

Forest Fires

Forest fires can start
when the weather is very hot
and dry. Special airplanes and helicopters
are used to put out these fires. A tank
full of water is carried underneath the
airplane or helicopter. A **pilot**
uses special controls to
open the tank and
release the water.

As this Firehawk
helicopter flies
over the forest, it
drops water onto
the fire below.

Firefighters also use helicopters to rescue people or animals from hard-to-reach places.

This rescue crew is riding in a mountain-rescue helicopter to lift a dog to safety.

Airport Accidents

Special equipment is needed to fight fires at airports. This is because airplanes are very big and can be filled with hundreds of people.

Airport fire trucks are built to put out fires on airplanes and to rescue any **passengers** trapped on board a plane.

This airport fire truck has special lights at the front so the driver can see through thick smoke.

Harbor Fireboats

Many boats use the **harbor** in New York City every day. They carry lots of **goods** and people from place to place. If a fire starts, the New York City Fire Department has a special boat named *Firefighter* that is sent to the rescue.

Fireboats have extra-long hoses and big water tanks. Firefighters use them to put out fires quickly and to stop them from spreading.

Fireboats can pump a lot of water onto a fire and can rescue both people and goods.

Other harbors have fireboats, too. They put out fires on ships and rescue passengers.

Ocean **Rescue**

Rescue workers use lifeboats and helicopters to help people who are in trouble at sea. If the water is fairly calm, they use lifeboats to carry people to safety.

A helicopter arrives to rescue people from a sinking boat.

If the water is too rough for lifeboats, rescuers use helicopters to **hoist** people to a safe place.

Send an Ambulance!

If a person has been badly **injured** or suddenly becomes very ill, someone calls for help. Rescue workers inside an ambulance turn on its flashing lights and loud siren. Then they rush to help the person, or take him or her to a hospital.

Inside an ambulance, there is a bed on wheels, medical equipment, and a place for the paramedics to sit.

Some places are difficult to reach by road. An air-ambulance helicopter is used instead.

Paramedics are men and women who are trained to take care of sick or injured people.

Police on the Way!

Police cars are very fast and can race to the scene of a crime or an accident. Police officers are trained to drive at high speeds on busy roads and highways.

Police cars have computers that officers use to check information, such as if a car is stolen.

Sometimes the police use a helicopter to chase people on the roads who are speeding or have committed a crime.

Motorcycle Patrol

In very crowded cities, some police officers ride motorcycles to reach accidents quickly or to chase people who may have broken the law.

Sometimes motorcycle police travel with the cars of important people to keep them safe.

Motorcycle police always wear safety helmets and are specially trained to ride their motorcycles.

Activities

- Start your own picture collection of emergency vehicles. Group them together by type—ambulances, fire engines, police cars, and so on.

- Can you tell what each of the emergency vehicles below is used for?

- Draw a picture of your favorite emergency vehicle. Make up a story to go with it. Say why it is your favorite.

- Look at the emergency vehicles below. Can you find the one that a police officer would drive?

Glossary

goods
Things that are bought and sold.

harbor
A place where ships and boats collect their goods or pick up and drop off people.

hoist
To pull someone or something up using a rope.

injured
When someone has been hurt.

paramedics
The men and women who drive an ambulance and care for injured people.

passengers
People who travel inside a vehicle.

pilot
A person who flies planes and/or helicopters.

siren
A gadget on an emergency vehicle that makes a loud noise.

vehicle
A machine that moves over land, in water, or through the sky.

Index